C000108107

IMAGES OF ENGLAND

Around Wilton

Flooding brought chaos to South Street a few days before Christmas in 1979. The wettest December night on record saw the River Nadder burst its banks and flooded the street for 300 yards. Although the flooding was serious, this resident was helped to safety by members of the local fire brigade.

Around Wilton

Chris Rousell

NONSUCH

Ditchampton in the early 1900s. All the houses on the left are still in situ today and with a few exceptions much remains the same. The row of houses in the centre have been replaced by new modern flats built in recent years. This area suffered badly in the floods of December 1910.

First published 2001
This new pocket edition 2006
Images unchanged from first edition

Nonsuch Publishing Limited
The Mill, Brimscombe Port,
Stroud, Gloucestershire, GL5 2QG
www.nonsuch-publishing.com

Nonsuch Publishing is an imprint of Tempus Publishing Group

British Library Cataloguing in Publication Data.
A catalogue record for this book is available from the British Library.

ISBN 1-84588-336-5

Typesetting and origination by Nonsuch Publishing Limited
Printed in Great Britain by Oaklands Book Services Limited

Contents

Acknowledgements

I would like to thank the following individuals for their help and assistance during the preparation of this publication: Mr Nick Griffiths, Curator of the Wilton Town Museum, for allowing me unrestricted access to the museum's photographic collection, without whose generous help, this publication would not have been possible. Mrs Marcia Holley and Mrs Nancy Morland, for their assistance with some items of information; Mrs Mary Hawley for the use of a photograph of her as Queen Elizabeth I in an early pageant; Mr Tony Peto for photographs of the *Devon Belle*; and from the *Salisbury Journal* editor, David Eidlestein and news editor, David Vallis for the use of some photographs in their files.

South Street around 1950 faces the market place and the junction with the A30. A large housing estate has since been built in the Bulbridge area and South Street has become a main access route for the estate and the Wilton First School.

Introduction

The market town of Wilton, reputed to be the second oldest borough in the country, is situated three miles west of Salisbury, nestling at the head of the Wylye and Nadder Valleys. Their respective rivers flow through the town, which can proudly trace its origins to Saxon times. The first settlers to establish themselves in the area, were a Saxon tribe known as the Wil-Sateas, but it wasn't long before the town grew, becoming a home for Saxon kings and the capital of Wessex. After King Alfred defeated the Danes, it became an important religious centre, dominated by an abbey. Here Saxon princesses and daughters of noblemen received their education, including Edith, the daughter of King Edgar and Wulfrith. Edith devoted her life to God at the abbey, but tragically died of a fever aged twenty-three years old. Because of her good works, she was later canonised, becoming the town's Patron Saint. At the dissolution, the abbey and its extensive lands were given, by Henry VIII, to the Earl of Pembroke. He demolished the abbey, and built Wilton House on the site, which is still the family seat to this day. The town has fifteen Royal Charters, the earliest dated 1100 granted by Henry I, the latest by Queen Victoria in 1885, when the borough boundary was extended. A new Corporation was elected, continuing in this format until local government reorganisation in 1974. Government of the town was taken over by the newly formed Salisbury District Council, at which time, the town lost its borough status. The office of Town Mayor continued, keeping alive a tradition dating back to 1265.

Wilton enjoyed great economic importance in the early years, helped by a wide variety of crafts, markets and fairs. However, by the end of the thirteenth century, the growth of Salisbury ended Wilton's prosperity leading to decline and decay. The only real survivor was the textile industry, in particular, weaving. These affairs continued until the start of the eighteenth century, along with the birth of the carpet industry, which developed from the weaving industry and became the town's salvation. Later, felt making was also established, with the opening of a mill in Crow Lane. Prosperity was fully established once again in the nineteenth century, helped by the arrival of the railway, unique in that the town was served by two stations, the Great Western Railway and the London and South Western Railway. An abundance of shops were selling merchandise of every description and new trades were introduced. Leisure activities were served by many societies and clubs, children's needs being catered for by clubs and societies run by the Methodist and Congregational churches.

Despite this prosperity, there was a poor community, whose survival relied on the help from regular payments from the poor relief fund. These were made possible by generous benefactors, collectively setting up various charities providing help from the cradle to the grave. Education was given at the Wilton Free School, catering for twenty poor boys of the parish, with a Dame School in Wilton Park catering for the needs of thirty-five poor girls. Later a National School was established in West Street.

The parish church served the religious needs for those of the Church of England faith, while for non-conformists, needs were looked after by the Methodist and Congregational churches, which flourished in the second half of the century.

Life wasn't always serious, there were occasions when inhabitants let their hair down, such as the Foresters August Bank holiday fête in Wilton Park, or celebrations commemorating the new Charter and the Golden and Diamond Jubilees of Queen Victoria. The first year of the twentieth century saw inhabitants celebrating in fine style, the 800th anniversary of the granting of the first charter.

The twentieth century was to endure two world wars in which Wilton and its inhabitants were inevitably involved. During the First World War Wilton played host to Australian soldiers, who were training on Salisbury Plain for front line duties in France. Many friendships between Wilton families and the soldiers were formed. Soon after the commencement of the Second World War, evacuees from Portsmouth arrived here; Southern Command was established, the headquarters of which were in Wilton House. The carpet factory ceased making carpets, turning to help the war effort by washing army blankets and making camouflage, kitbags and tarpaulins. American Forces also established a camp in the Avenue, many of whom were billeted with local families who readily made them welcome.

After the war the town slowly returned to normal, trying to pick up the pieces, but there were still many shortages which continued for a long period after the war's end. Only at that time did the carpet factory commence making carpets once more. However, some changes soon took place. A new council housing estate was built on an area of farming land in the Wishford Road, soon to be followed by further housing development on a much larger scale in the Bulbridge area. This consisted of both council and private development. Later, homes for officers, serving at the army headquarters in the Avenue, were built at the top end of this estate.

By the mid 1960s, the town had seen the closure of both its railway stations. This, coupled with the popularity of the car and frequent bus services, once again saw the town losing out to Salisbury. The advent of supermarkets brought about the gradual closure of local grocers shops and butchers, along with many other retail outlets which suffered a reduction in trade. Some were forced to close down.

The town suffered its biggest shock with the closure of the carpet factory in March 1995, but thanks to a management buyout a few weeks later, the factory was reopened. Once again, carpet making, for which Wilton is noted, began to flourish even if it was now operating on a smaller scale.

The rest of the factory site has been redeveloped as a retail shopping village, which opened in November 1997 with a blaze of publicity.

Originally this complex housed the carpet factory museum and the town museum run by the Wilton Historical Society. Unfortunately, during 2004, economic forces, plus a fall in visitor numbers, meant that the carpet factory could not sustain the costs for its own museum, or those for the town museum which it had generously supported. To date, the town museum is still without a home, but hopefully in the not too distant future perhaps the opportunity will once again present itself.

Fortunately, the town itself has a great abundance of historical sites worth visiting, Wilton House obviously being one of them, but steps must be taken to make sure that these sites are firmly established on the toursts' itinerary.

One

Around the Town

The Old Wool Loft. This rather imposing building once stood in the centre of Wilton, at the western end of the market, known to Wiltonians as Four Corners. Its main use was as a warehouse and was demolished in the early 1920s to make way for extensions to the market place. This photograph, taken by the author's grandfather in the late 1800s, views the building from the old market place. Adjacent are some of the houses which once stood in this area, while on the left are the premises of the present day Lloyds TSB Bank, the frontage of which has hardly changed for over a century.

From the roof of the Co-op building, this birds-eye view of the area behind the Wool Loft shows the houses that once occupied this area of the town. Eventually they fell into decay and along with the Wool Loft, were demolished, making way for the market extension and enhancement scheme. The road between the houses and St Mary's churchyard on the right was known as Brede Street.

The original market place in the early 1900s. The ancient market cross dominates this early scene, which in very early times represented a symbol of fair trading at markets. One unusual feature is that the cross is topped with a sundial. Another use for the cross was that it acted as a platform for the reading of Royal Proclamations, as well as being a site for the old town crier. The thatched cottage was the office of F. Whatley, a coal and coke merchant; behind which can be seen the Greyhound Inn, which dates from the eighteenth century and was formerly a posting house.

The Town Hall. The date 1736 is engraved on one of the stone window sills, but it is generally accepted that this date relates to the restoration, rather than its actual building. It was the home of the town council, until 1948-49, when it moved to a new location in Kingsbury Square, but it remained open for public functions until the opening of the new community centre in 1978. Its conversion to a Baptist chapel took place during the 1980s. The clock commemorates the Golden Jubilee of Queen Victoria and was unveiled by Lord Pembroke in 1888.

New Market Place. The newly erected Memorial to Sidney, 14th Earl of Pembroke and Montgomery, now dominates the new market place area, with only the area around it waiting to be resurfaced. The Memorial was paid for by public subscription and unveiled on 21 May 1924. The tall building behind the Memorial is the Co-op and it can clearly be seen that the thatched cottage of F. Whatley, the coal merchant, is now tiled and the business sign has been removed. It is now a private residence.

Market Place. Despite the bus stop being located by the churchyard wall, the Memorial served as the setting down and picking up point for bus travellers making the journey between the town and Salisbury. Due to the increasing popularity of the motor car, the Memorial was removed during the 1960s to accommodate better parking facilities in the town centre.

Built in 1867, the Wilton and District Co-op stores, served Wiltonians and people from many of the surrounding villages for just over one hundred years. Built on the site of the original carpet factory, it was now making way for another development, the Wilton Health Centre, which opened in 1979. The picture was taken at the start of demolition, which also included the two cottages to the right.

Kingsbury Square just after the turn of the nineteenth century showing just how safe it was to take an afternoon stroll in the road, despite a footpath being provided on the left. Today such a scene would be impossible. Kingsbury Square is said to have acquired this name because it is in the area where Wessex kings established their palaces, the word 'Kingsbury' meaning, 'the stronghold of the king'.

This photograph of Kingsbury Square follows about thirty years after the previous one. Evidence of more road traffic is shown by white lines painted in the centre of the road, which is now tarmac instead of packed earth. The gas lamp on the right has disappeared and a signpost is now in evidence on the corner of the grass verge.

At the western end of Kingsbury Square once stood this impressive building, the Talbot and Wyvern Hall, better known locally as the Coffee Tavern. The foundation stone was laid in 1873 by Sir Edmund Antrobus, MP for Wilton. It was the headquarters of the Wilton Total Abstinence Society and as at this time one-sixth of the town's population were teetotal, it became a popular venue for all ages. Many events were held here, including in December 1919, a prize-giving ceremony for pupils of the Wilton Free School. The hall was demolished in 1965 to make way for a new Georgian-style house.

Kingsbury Square, looking towards Bell Lane and the market place. The house on the extreme left was at one time Miss Smith's School for Young Ladies. Just past the Talbot and Wyvern Hall, the house with ivy covering its walls, has some of the windows bricked up. The most possible explanation for this was because reducing the number of windows reduced payments of 'window tax' which once existed a few centuries ago.

PRIMITIVE METHODIST CHURCH,
WILTON.

A **BAZAAR** AND
SALE OF WORK

in aid of the

CENTENARY THANKSGIVING FUND

will be held in the

TALBOT & WYVERN HALL,

(kindly lent by the Earl of Pembroke),

On Wednesday & Thursday, Oct. 21st. & 22nd, 1908.

OPENING CEREMONIES AT 3 p.m.

The Bazaar will be opened on the First Day
by
MRS. L. L. MORSE, of Swindon.

Chairman - G. BILLETT, Esq.

Supported by L. L. MORSE Esq., M.P., Alderman
John Moore, Revs. J. H. Green, W. T. Healey,
G. L. Roberts, R. W. Gair, and T. Hunter.

The Bazaar will be opened on the Second Day
by
THE MAYORESS OF WILTON.

Chairman - H. G. GREGORY, Esq., J.P.

Supported by His Worship the Mayor of Wilton,
the Deputy Mayor, Ald. E. Slow, Revs. F.
Shergold, T. C. Rigg, G. L. Roberts and
T. Hunter.

Wilton Printing Works, North St.

This bazaar and sale of work held at the Talbot and Wyvern Hall by the Wilton Primitive
Methodist church was held to help raise funds for the Primitive Methodist Centenary
Thanksgiving Fund, which was attempting to raise £250,000 nationally. The portion to be
raised by the Salisbury District was £350. Besides many stalls there was also entertainment
and competitions.

F. WHATLEY,

Coal and Coke Merchant,

MARKET PLACE,

~ ~ ~ WILTON.

BEST COAL SUPPLIED————

AT

————LOWEST POSSIBLE PRICES.

SPECIAL QUOTATION FOR TRUCK LOADS.

BRIQUETTES KEPT IN STOCK.

Whatley's advertisements, 1898. The name of Whatley was associated for many years with the coal merchants business in the town. At the time this advertisement appeared, the firm would have been collecting its coal from the London and South Western station, and delivering it to customers with the aid of a horse and cart.

Garland's Dairy, 1898. At this period milk would not have been delivered in bottles, as it is today, but would have been brought to the doorstep in churns. This would have been mounted on a two wheel type trolley, and the measured amount of milk was taken from the churn with a ladle. The contents were then poured into the customer's jug, or another utensil they might have used. It is interesting to note that customers could receive two deliveries a day, if they wished to.

Wilton Dairy,

~* KINGSBURY SQUARE, WILTON. *~

(Entrance in Greyhound Lane.)

ARTHUR GARLAND, Proprietor.

MILK, CREAM, BUTTER, AND EGGS FRESH DAILY.

FAMILIES WAITED ON TWICE DAILY.

ALL ORDERS RECEIVE PROMPT AND PERSONAL ATTENTION.

POULTRY TO ORDER   A TRIAL ORDER SOLICITED.

Old Market Place. The large house on the right, looking towards the churchyard of St Mary's church, is the Old Rectory of the former parish church. It was built in the eighteenth century, but is thought to be part of an older house. Evidence of this is shown on a map dated 1586, but parts of the rectory appear to be of even older origin. In the distance, appearing above a tree top, is the bell tower of the parish church in West Street.

The Pembroke Arms and Hotel. Originally, the hotel was built to cater for visitors to Wilton House, which was directly opposite. The reason for this is that before 1840, the road between the hotel and the roundabout at the junction of the A36; which leads up to the house and the A30 was not in existence. In 1841, the local office of the Customs and Excise were housed in the hotel, the words are still visible today on the side of the hotel facing towards the roundabout. In 1870, when the Wiltshire Archaeological Society held a meeting in the town, they partook of a meal here.

In its heyday the hotel was so popular that it needed an annexe. Which today is a private house known as Minster Cottage.

This riverside walk on the main road opposite Wilton House was very popular with residents in the early part of the twentieth century. In this photograph, Island House can clearly be seen, formally the home of Col. Crichton Maitland, a former chairman of the local magistrates. Both he and his wife took a very active part in the affairs of the town and the church and the house gardens were frequently used for fêtes. Today the trees have grown much taller and the house is not so clearly visible.

This view from the early 1900s looks back towards the view on the previous photograph. Wilton House is to the left and to this day, has a wonderful display of daffodils each spring; which form a lovely yellow carpet among the trees.

To the left is the roadway leading to the main entrance of Wilton House, watched over by the statue of the Earl of Pembroke, complete with his sword. Today the sword is no longer with him. It was removed during the Second World War by some American servicemen as a souvenir of their visit to the town; the act was witnessed by a young resident of the town. The main road into Wilton is on the right.

Taken from the other side of the bridge, this splendid scene at the entrance to Wilton house, is familiar to visitors today and looks, in many respects, as though very little has changed. To the left of the main entrance is the visitors' entrance leading through to the souvenir shop. The pavement continues over the bridge on both sides, making it safer for pedestrians who have to contend with the modern traffic.

The Recreation Ground opened in May 1912 and soon became a popular venue for all ages. As well as a play area, a bowling green and a pleasant riverside walk were provided for the older generations to enjoy. Later, a tennis court was added to cater for those who wished to spend their leisure hours in a more energetic manner. The stone seat near the bowling green is a memorial to King Edward VII, who made a visit to Wilton four years earlier. The seat was unveiled by the Countess of Pembroke and the Recreation Ground was opened by the Earl of Pembroke.

The Crossroads at the turn of the nineteenth century was an ideal spot for a mother and baby and a gentleman to take a rest. For many decades after, it was a popular venue for residents to sit and as they used to say, 'watch the world go by'. The houses in the background are Magdalene Trust almshouses.

The Avenue in the early 1900s. This approach into Wilton was cut during the 1840s, a period when many people had fallen on hard times. It is generally thought that the Pembroke family instigated the making of the road and tree planting, as a means of offering employment to those in need and helping to ease their desperate situation.

In earlier years the Wheatsheaf Inn was famed for making its own beer and was well patronised by shepherds attending the Wilton Sheep Fair. One of their customs was to hold an annual contest to determine who would bear the title of 'King of the Shepherds'. This took the form of a great fight, in which it appears weapons were used, but the nature of the weapons used in the combat has not been recorded. On that night the shepherds slept on the floor of the inn, lying in a rough circle, each man with his head on his dog, using it as a pillow. This relationship was two-fold, the shepherd guarded his dog, his most valuable property, whilst the dog guarded his master's belongings.

Two

Schools

The National School in 1912 was situated in West Street. It was originally a parochial school, becoming a day school in 1842, uniting with the National Society in 1902. Wide collars seemed to be the order of the day for the young pupils, but even more interesting is that two of the boys in the front row are wearing lace collars.

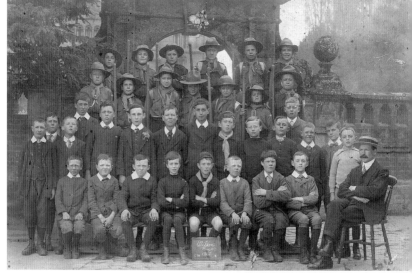

Above: Wilton Park School, *c.*1860. Mrs Sidney Herbert, Lady Herbert of Lea, provided education for poor girls in her Church of England School for Girls, in a converted baroque pavilion situated in Wilton Park; which subsequently became known as 'Wilton Park School'. The main craft taught was needlework, at which pupils became specialists and some became involved with marking and making Wilton House Linen. Such were their skills, on leaving school the girls were in great demand as under-nurses and sewing maids. When each girl left school they were given a box of clothes, which were home made. The box itself was made of wood grown on the estate and made at the sawmills. The religious part of their education included learning by heart passages from the Bible, singing hymns and making notes of sermons preached at Wilton church.

Opposite above: The National School, *c.*1910. Accommodation was provided for 310 pupils, including infants. Originally only boys were taught, but late in the 1800s girls were admitted. Mistresses taught the infants and their male colleagues, the older children.

Opposite below: The National School in 1915 and an occasion for Mr Long the master to wear a straw boater hat, the height of men's fashion around this period.

Park School in the early 1900s. This picture of pupils of a later period, shows them posing for a photograph outside the main entrance to the school.

Park School in the early 1900s. Just exactly what the Wilton Park schoolgirls are celebrating is not indicated. Perhaps it is a celebration of the former Empire Day, judging by the show of patriotism. It is likely that three hearty cheers are being given, as the boys on the right from the Wilton Free School have their caps raised in the air.

Wilton Free School in the late 1900s. The school opened in 1714, founded by Walter Dyer, who left £600 in a will to be used to establish a school in the town for twenty poor boys of the parish. The boys were taught to read and write, grounded in the rules of common arithmetic and instructed in the principles and doctrines of the Church of England. The school in North Street is now a private house.

Wilton Free School in 1914. Pupils of the school pose for a picture taken for the school's 200th Anniversary Celebrations, all of them resplendent in their military school uniforms, for which they were sometimes ridiculed when they wore them in the street. The gentleman on the extreme left is the headmaster John Coates. His wife makes an appearance on the right.

Wilton Senior School in the late 1930s. September 1935 saw the opening of the Wilton Church of England Senior Mixed School in the Hollows. The Headmaster Mr Gus Elliott was, by all accounts, a strict disciplinarian. This is recollected in a short rhyme made up by some of the pupils, 'Gus Elliott goes to church on Sunday, to pray to God to give him strength, to whack the boys on Monday'. Children came to the school from many surrounding villages, as well as Wilton, where they received a good basic education prior to leaving to take up full time employment. In the late 1940s the name changed to Wilton Area Secondary Modern School, retaining the name until government changes in education policy in 1975, when it became Wilton Middle School. Mr Gus Elliott can be seen in the centre of the back row. Unfortunately the school closed in July 2005, when the local education authority decided to revert to the former two-tier system of education, which it had abandoned in June 1975 for the the three-tier system, in which it became a middle school. Its complete closure came as a shock, angering many residents and parents in the community. Despite protests and a public meeting, authorities had made up their minds, the school closing at the end of the summer term. Plans and suggestions as to its further use are at the present time under review, but nothing definite has yet been decided.

Miss Wright's Preparatory School in 1945. This was a private school situated at the top of North Street in a thatched house. Here, young boys and girls received their early education, prior to going to a state school. Miss Wright was the headmistress and Mrs Blandford was her assistant. Even in 1945, the schoolroom was quite reminiscent of Victorian times because Miss Wright was to all accounts quite a fearsome character.

Wilton Primary School probably in the late 1930. Some of the girls from the school pose to have a photograph taken in the girls' playground. This was separated from the boys' playground at the front end of the school by the toilet block. It is most likely that during this period Miss Drake was the Headmistress.

The town in 1754 looks small in comparison to the vast area of Wilton Park and the grounds of Wilton House. In the bottom right, St Mary's church and the market place are clearly visible, as well as Crow Lane. The square looking feature across the market place to the left of the church, is the original carpet factory, which was owned by Moody and Barford. This was on the site of the present health centre and adjoining car park. The short stretch of road, which leads from the market place to Kingsbury Square, was known as Carpet Walk; which can be seen quite clearly on the map. At this period the road stopped just after Russell Street, only reverting to a through road in the 1840s.

Three

Weather

Serious flooding in December 1910 occurred in the Ditchampton area. The flooding followed heavy rains which caused torrents of water to rush in from the downs. The cellars of the Bell Inn were badly affected and barrels of beer were floating around in the water.

The depth of water in Ditchampton was sufficient to support a boat and stretched from the railway bridge in the distance, past the Bell Inn and almost to the church. Many residents were forced to live upstairs until the waters subsided, one resident fitted a platform in the kitchen so food could be prepared without standing in icy cold water.

Five years later in 1915 more serious flooding occurred when both the Ditchampton and North Street areas were badly affected. At the market end of North Street the whole length of the street was covered in water.

Further up North Street, again in 1915, the water was much deeper and supported a man actually rowing a boat. This was possible on the left hand side because the street is a little lower than the other. Also, properties on this side suffered more than those on the opposite side. Planks were arranged and supported above the water to enable people to get about where the water was at its deepest.

During the 1915 flooding, St John's Square featured an arrangement of planks being used here by two men in an effort to keep their feet dry.

The flooding in Russell Street, in 1915, stretched from the junction with the main road. It was reported that during the flooding, an eel was seen swimming in the water.

A very unusual picture of Russell Street in 1915 seen from the junction with North Street. Here the water flows into the street in quite a torrent.

Wearing his familiar white apron, Mr Sinca the grocer and his wife, are open for business as usual, despite the flood waters entering their shop at Ditchampton in 1915. The name Sinca is unusual and the story concerning it stems back to his father, Simeon Sinca, who was brought to Wilton by Lord Pembroke in Victorian times; employing him as a house-carpenter at Wilton House. Simeon was a Slav and when he was a small boy aged about four or five years old, he and another boy strayed into the English lines two days before the bombardment of Sebastopol. Detained in the camp for their own safety during the bombardment, efforts after the event to find their parents failed, so two English soldiers adopted them, brought them home, gave them an education and taught them a trade. Not knowing their surnames, the soldiers gave them the fornames of Alma and Inkerman, but one of the boys couldn't pronounce the name Inkerman, so made it Sinca. From that time, until the end of his life, he þecame Sinca. He married a Wilton girl and settled here for the rest of his days.

The main gate of Wilton House in 1908. On 25 April of this year, a freak snowstorm hit Wilton, which prompted local printer and photographer Mr W. Jukes to trudge through the snowbound streets to record the event. At Wilton House he captured this Christmas card scene as trees were just coming into leaf, and weighed down by a thick layer of freshly fallen snow.

West Street in 1908. Apart from a track on the pavement and two on the road, the snowfall is mainly undisturbed. The tree on the left is bent over at a very steep angle with the weight of the snow and in the central distance, Grovely Downs can be seen bearing the white mantle, making the trees of the folly stand out against the white backdrop.

Despite a fairly heavy fall during the night of Saturday 9 January 1982 in West Street, modern traffic has almost eliminated the snow from the road.

Looking up North Street to Four Corners in 1982, the lying snow remains largely undisturbed unlike that on the busy A30 in the foreground. Wilton's famous Christmas tree is shown on the right.

After some heavy rain in 1990 the top end of North Street became flooded, water flowing from the River Wyle.

Extensive flooding occurred on the River Wyle just below the carpet factory, where two tributaries join the main river. The Recreation Ground was affected, in 1995, as far as the bowling green, making it impossible to walk along the adjoining path without rubber boots. The area behind the bowls club was also extensively affected by the flood waters.

Four

Carpet Factory

When the factory had completed a prestige order for a customer, the finished carpet was often displayed to full effect on the lawn of the historic courtyard. However, there is no indication of the customer for whom this magnificent carpet was designed and displayed at the carpet factory in the early 1900s. In the background is the factory manager's house, which was the first private house in the town to have electric light in 1911.

Five weavers pose for a photograph in the Wilton Shed of the carpet factory in the late 1800s. The weaver second from left, sitting behind the wheel on the loom, is the author's grandfather, William James Lane, who throughout his working life, immersed himself in many activities of the town. The names of the others in the picture are not known but, likeWilliam Lane they would have spent years training for their trade, which was very much respected in those times. The weavers' rights were protected, by a Charter from King William III enabling them to form a corporate body and granting them powers to issue certificates to all those who had served seven year apprenticeships. Weavers had to be elected to this guild, paying a subscription when elected. Much later this body became more generally known as 'The Weavers Guild'. This Charter, in effect, protected the weavers by prohibiting all persons who were not licensed by them, from carrying on a similar business within four miles of Wilton.

Witton Carpet Factory
February 7th 1884.

I Josiah Jacobs, hereby Certify that William Lane has this day completed his term of Service as Second Loom Weaver, and having paid all demands, is now entitled to all rights & privileges as belonging to the Trade.

Josiah Jacobs.
Secretary to Witton Carpet
Weavers Association.

Dated Feb 7/84

This certificate from 1884 was presented to William Lane when he became a fully fledged weaver. Originally it would have had two waxed seals attached to it, but the marks on this certificate clearly show where they were attached. Josiah Jacobs was William's father-in-law.

Wilton carpet Factory in the 1920s. The dyeing of the wool for the carpets was done at the factory, which was an exacting process. All the different colours had to be dyed one batch at a time, so sufficient yarn needed to be processed to enable the colour to remain the same, as it would be impossible to make a new batch of dye to exactly the same colour. Today the yarn is bought in and hand dyeing is now a lost craft at the factory.

Creating the designs for carpets was a very important part of the process of carpet making. Often as not, customers would indicate the type of design they required when placing a specialised order for a hotel, cinema or theatre foyer etc. This would mean that the customer and design department would have a close working relationship. For retail, sale carpet designs would be planned between designers and factory management.

Once a design was agreed, it would then be drawn and painted with water colours. A small sample would be made to check the design could be woven correctly and to give a good indication as to how the complete carpet would look using the yarn dyed in the colours used by the designer.

A most unusual order was received by the factory during the 1930s from Dame Laura Knight, who was famous for her paintings, especially those of circus subjects. She asked the factory if they would make two carpets, the designs of which were based on copies of her paintings, one of Pirou and Columbine, the other of Neptune surrounded by water nymphs and sea creatures. Always ready to meet a challenge, the factory's design team managed to resolve the many problems that the order presented. One difficult problem to overcome was that of scale, reproducing the paintings on carpets measuring twenty-four feet square. Eventually all problems were overcome and a faithful reproduction of both carpets was made.

The carpet factory, *c.*1910. The historic courtyard certainly didn't give the impression that this was part of the carpet factory complex, even though the buildings housed offices and showrooms. These buildings on the right date back to the seventeenth century. The little girl seen on the lawn could well be the daughter of the factory manager.

This is the scene in the former Wilton Shed, recorded a few days after the shock announcement of the closure of the factory by new owners Carpets International in 1995. Weaving carpets in this shed had ceased much earlier and it was now being used more as a store. Today, this shed has been fully restored and is now the ladies outfitting department of the Edinburgh Woolen Mill, one of the shops in the Wilton Shopping Village, established in late 1997.

Right: The whole town was devastated by the news of the factory closure in January 1995, and the news was made worse when it was announced that in future all Wilton Royal carpets would be made at their Bradford factory. To add insult to injury, this meant that the Wilton factory would loose its Royal Warrant, which it had proudly held since 1905.

Below: Not long after the closure in March 1995, these signs disappeared forever, but this photographic record serves as a reminder of the factory's former status. On the day of the closure, the workers proudly walked through the gates for the last time and as one Wilton resident put it, 'Wilton died on that day'. However, about two months later the factory reopened on a smaller scale, thanks to a management buy-out and the remainder of the site was developed into the Wilton Shopping Village.

THE PATENT OFFICE: TRADE MARKS BRANCH.

LONDON, *4 th July* 1905.

Gentlemen,

    I beg to inform you, pursuant to Rule 35 of the Trade Marks Rules, 1890, that the Trade Mark No. *271303*, advertised in the *Trade Marks Journal,* No. *1417*, has been registered in your name   for the following goods in Class *36*, viz.:— *Carpets*

    The Registration dates from the *21st* day of *March* 1905.

         I am,

         Gentlemen,

         Your obedient Servant,

The Wilton Royal Carpet Factory Company Limited

                C. N. DALTON,

                COMPTROLLER-GENERAL.

REPRESENTATION OF TRADE MARK AS ADVERTISED.—THIS REPRODUCES IN SUBSTANCE THE MATERIAL FEATURES OF THE MARK AS IT APPEARS ON THE REGISTER.

This is a copy of the document from the Patent Office, registering the carpet factory Trade Mark in 1905. This trade mark was used by the carpet factory, in conjunction with the warrant issued in the same year. At that time the factory was known as. 'The Wilton Royal Carpet Factory Limited'.

Five

Wilton at Night

During the 1950s Howard Cooke a local businessman and Justice of the Peace, produced some fascinating pictures of Wilton by night. In St John's Square he captured part of St John's Priory church on the right, plus some of the houses opposite. The only source of lighting was a street lamp on the corner.

The approach to Kingsbury Square, seen from the car park of the Pembroke Arms Hotel, shows a glimpse into the Square which is framed by Wilton Park wall on the left and houses on the right. The Talbot and Wyvern Hall can just be made out in the middle distance.

In the foreground is the main road between the town centre and the roundabout at Fugglestone with the background detail of Kingsbury Square.

The shadows of the lime trees in Kingsbury Square are cast onto the two doorways and give an impression that ivy, or some other trailing plant is growing on the walls. Attractive details of the brick work is visible.

Looking towards the corner of Kingsbury Square is the road which leads to the Pembroke Arms Hotel. The house on the extreme right once housed a post office. Exactly when this was isn't known, although the words 'Post Office' can still be seen painted on the wall, but are now faded by time.

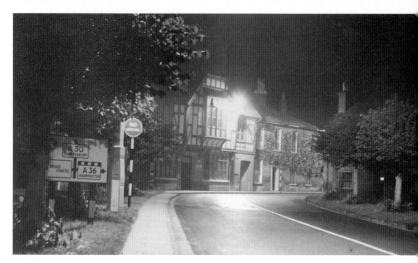

This final shot of Kingsbury Square shows the road turning the corner into the market place, the road sign clearly indicating the directions for motorists at the road junction ahead. To the left on the corner is the Talbot and Wyvern Hall, its frontage partially blotted out by the street light suspended from its structure.

Howard Cooke only had to walk outside his gate to take this night time winter scene of Shaftesbury Road in February 1954. Such is the quality of the photograph that even the snow on the boughs of the trees stands out well against the black night sky.

Six

Events and Occasions

The announcement of an election result in the early 1920s. Crowds gather outside the town hall awaiting to hear the result of the Parliamentary Election, most likely for the South Wiltshire Division. Next door is the town's fire station, the words on the door just being visible to the right of the gentleman on horseback.

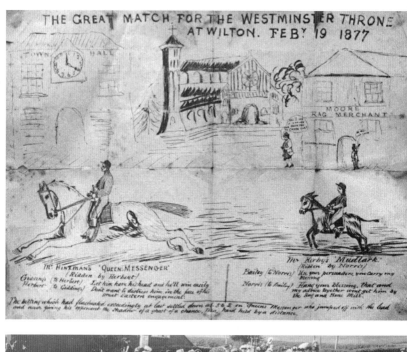

THE GREAT MATCH FOR THE WESTMINSTER THRONE
AT WILTON. FEB.Y 19 1877

The Departure of the King & Queen from Wilton. F. Futcher, Photo.

Above: The King and Queen left Wilton House in 1908, for the London and South Western Railway station at Wilton, where they embarked on the royal train for the journey back to London. The station was specially decorated for the occasion with plants in the window boxes grown by the station master. There was a touching moment during the departure concerning the blind daughter of the station master. As the queen walked past the nine-year old girl, the Countess of Pembroke asked the station master's wife to bring her daughter forward, then commenced to inform the queen how the girl had only been inflicted with her blindness since March of that year and that it had been diagnosed as incurable. The Queen then took the girl's hand, kissed her and said, 'My poor dear child, God Bless You', then her majesty turned to the daughter of Lady Beatrix Wilson, and joined that child's hand to the other child and said, 'Take care of this poor little girl', after which she spoke a few words of sympathy to the station master's wife. (Photograph by Futcher of Salibury).

Opposite above: In January 1877, Sir Edmund Antrobus retired as Wilton's MP, having represented the Borough in Parliament for twenty years without opposition. February saw an election to represent the Borough between the Hon. Sidney Herbert and J.S. Norris. Herbert won by a very large majority, polling 751 votes, against the 187 polled for Norris. After the election this cartoon was produced, stating that betting on 'Queen's Messenger' had settled down at five to two, giving him the lead and not giving his opponent a chance.

Opposite below: On the weekend of 27 June 1908, King Edward VII and Queen Alexandra made a private visit to the Earl and Countess of Pembroke at Wilton house. After arriving at Salisbury station, the King and Queen drove in an open carriage to Wilton. On arrival they were greeted by the mayor who, on behalf of Wilton inhabitants and children, presented the King with two sepia drawings of Wilton House and the town hall.

Coronation of King George V. Celebration at Wilton.
June 22nd 1911.

Coronation of King George V. Celebration at Wilton. June 22nd 1911.

Above: A bonfire to celebrate the Silver Jubilee of King George V in 1935. Unfortunately the name of the person standing in front of the huge bonfire, is not given on the original photograph. Most likely, he was one of the people concerned with its building. The setting is Grovely Down, the location, Jubilee Field and it appears that the bonfire was set near to the Jubilee Oak tree which commemorated the jubilee of Queen Victoria. There was, on this occasion like many others in a similar vein, a torchlight procession from the town to the bonfire, which would have been lit from one of the torches. In Victorian times and up to just after the Second World War, Wilton was well known for its torchlight processions and bonfires. In Victorian Wilton the torches were made at the Felt Mills, and the ingredients were sheep's wool saturated in tar or any other inflammable material. Unfortunately, as the torches burned down, pieces of burning material would tend to fly off, sometimes landing among the crowd, making them scatter very quickly! It is said that the line of torches wending their way up Grovely Hill, made quite an impressive sight when viewed from West Street.

Opposite above: Celebrations for the coronation of King George V in 1911. There was nothing like a special royal event to get Wilton inhabitants to let their hair down and celebrate in fine style. At this time, the country still had an Empire that it was proud of and this float in a procession is based on that theme. Also represented are the English characters of John Bull and Britannia.

Opposite below: Coronation celebrations in 1911. Inhabitants of the town enjoyed themselves in the old market place, on what would seem to be a nice summer's day. The umbrellas are being used to keep off the sun, not rain!

Above: Leaving the parish church on Rememberence Sunday in 1946, the mayoral procession makes its way back to the council chambers, after the annual Service of Remembrance. From left to right: Revd J.J. Haynes, mayor's chaplain, who in the previous year had taken over as the minister of the Congregational church in Crow Lane alongside Mr Leopold Lush, town clerk; the Countess of Pembroke, now Deputy Mayor, accompanied by who is thought to be the General Officer Commanding for Southern Command and Mr Brown, the macebearer.

Opposite above: Edith Maud Olivier made history by being elected Wilton's first lady mayor in 1938. The daughter of Canon Dacres Olivier, a former rector of the town, she was also a well known author who wrote many books. The choice was popular with the residents, as she was loved by everyone and she loved them, spending many hours helping others. The photograph shows Miss Olivier walking in procession on the occasion of her Civic Service.

Opposite below: Procession to the Wartime Memorial in 1943. Wilton's second lady mayor was the Countess of Pembroke, who took up office in 1942 and remained until 1945. The reason for this long term in office, was due to the male councillors' other wartime duties which put any mayoral duties on hold. The procession is shown in the Avenue, where the council had temporary offices at Fugglestone House for the duration of the war. The building is one of the council houses, converted from First World War army hut on this former army camp site.

Left: In February 1953, a year after her accession to the throne, Queen Elizabeth II, accompanied by the Duke of Edinburgh, made a private visit to Wilton House. On Sunday they attended the church service and here the Duke is being introduced to the mayor, Aldermen Vincent Moore. The gentleman by his side is the Earl of Pembroke.

Below: This shows the Queen being introduced to Mrs Moore the mayoress on the royal visit in 1953. The lady with her back to the camera, is the Countess of Pembroke. Waiting at the entrance to the church is the rector, Revd William Drury, with the churchwarden standing close behind him. The streets of the town were packed with people anxious to catch sight of their new Queen, who was only about four months away from her Coronation.

Right: Reginald, 15th Earl of Pembroke, was a member of the town council and was elected mayor on two consecutive occasions during the time 1932-33. His wife, Beatrice, née Paget, also held the office of mayor during the 1950s. This photograph appeared on the mayoral christmas card and was most likely taken in the grounds of Wilton House.

Below: The Countess of Pembroke was inaugurated as the mayor for the fifth time in 1954, taking over the office from Alderman Vincent Moore, on the right. The Earl of Pembroke is seen on the left. Mrs Shergold the mayoress was serving her eighth time in this capacity, having been mayoress for the countess during the war years, then on three occasions for her husband Samuel in 1941 and again in 1955-56. This was a record achievement which no other mayoress to date has equalled.

Left: Mayor Graham Moody, reads out the Royal Proclamation announcing the accession of Queen Elizabeth II to the throne in 1952. Looking on from the platform outside the former town hall in the market place are from left to right: Revd J.J. Haynes, the mayor, town clerk Mr Leopold Lush and Mrs Joan Moody, mayoress. The gentleman wearing the top hat is one of the council macebearers. In the past Royal Proclamations have been read from the market cross, but it appears this tradition was not followed on this occasion.

Below: The mayor, Alderman V.H. Moore can be seen standing at the top table, speaking to guests attending this special lunch for the over sixties in 1953. Seated to his right is his wife, the mayoress. This was the second consecutive year that Alderman was elected mayor. He was asked to continue for this special year, due to his long service to public duty and his immense popularity. Wilton mayors are elected in May, which at times can lead to confusion as the mayoral years can overlap the calender years.

In 1948 Wilton Town Council moved from its original chambers in the town hall, to a Former Masonic Hall in Kingsbury Square. To celebrate the move, a dinner was held in the new chamber, hosted by the mayor, Mrs Caroline Stokes and her mayoress, Mrs Moore, who is on the extreme left. Guests standing at the top table are to the left of the mayor the mayor of Salisbury, to the right of the mayor, General Sir John Harding, General Officer in Command of the Southern Command and the Mayoress of Salisbury.

The mayor, Mr Albert Belk, with the town clerk, Mr Leopold Lush at his side, lead members of the town council to the parish church for the annual Civic Sunday in 1973. On this occasion, the town beadle was carrying the mace. This was the final year of the Borough Council, as the following year local government reforms came into being, allowing the newly formed Salisbury District Council to take over the town's affairs, reducing Wilton Council to parish status.

The final meeting of the borough council, in 1974, was presided by the retiring mayor, Mr Albert Belk. Standing on the left is Mrs Betty Belk, mayoress and the Rector of Wilton, Revd Denton White. The end of the borough council also brought about the closure of the council offices and the redundancy of the borough surveyor. The office of town clerk remained unaffected as did the office of mayor.

As a final gesture to the old borough council, seventeen of its past mayors were presented with certificates of recognition and commemoration of having served the office of mayor for the, now former, borough council. They are gathered around Mr Albert Belk in 1974, the last outgoing mayor of the old Boroughs of Wilton.

As a memorial to the Earl of Pembroke, who had died six years earlier, the drinking fountain was placed at the bottom of the Avenue at its junction with the Crossroads in 1901. The inauguration ceremony was performed by the succeeding Earl of Pembroke. The inscription around the bowl, which can still clearly be seen today reads, 'This fountain is given by Gertrude Countess of Pembroke in memory of happy days at Wilton. Trusting that it will be a comfort to all passers by and thirsty animals. 1901 AD'.

Written on the back of this photograph are the words, 'North Street, Called Moat House, therefore after closing of Free School'. This indicates that the photograph was taken after 1924, but exactly who is parading, or what the occasion was, is not clear.

An entry by the Women's Institute in a Wilton carnival, probably during the early to middle 1950s. It is obvious that the entry depicts women's dress of former years, with a little boy dressed in the uniform of the Wilton Free School.

Festival of Great Britain Celebrations 1951. The float just visible on the right, represents the town's early history connected with Wilton Abbey. The float is part of the Festival of Great Britain in 1951 and carries Mary Shergold, now Mrs Hawley, as Queen Elizabeth I. Mary also depicted Queen Elizabeth in the carnival of Coronation Year 1953.

On the completion of the procession in 1951, a pageant was performed depicting the town's history. This scene in the pageant is shows Queen Elizabeth I presenting Sir Walter Raleigh with a lock of her hair.

Wilton's first Carnival Week took place in September 1949, and Phyllis Turner was chosen to be the first Carnival Queen, photographed here watching a variety show with her attendants at the Michael Herbert Hall. Her crown was made by Horace Uphill, an extremely creative and inventive person, designing the crown as a replica of those worn by Wessex kings. He took only a week to make it. Fashioned out of wood and aluminium, it was decorated with ermine trimming enhanced by studding the fringe with rock crystals, imitation pearls, emeralds and turquoise and finished with a lining of red velvet. The crown is still worn by present day carnival queens. Richard Best, chairman of the carnival committee is on the left.

Inside the gates of Wilton House, after the procession through the streets. Horace Uphill, wearing the light suit, stands by another of his creations, two white swans pulling the float of the carnival queen, in 1950, The carnival queen was sixteen year old Eileen Hooker seen here with her attendants. The page seated in the front row, is eight year old Trevor Ford, who still lives and works in the town today. In order to be the page, Trevor had to get special permission from the head teacher of his school, as he was required to attend many of the evening events which went on into the late evening.

Wilton celebrated the Coronation of Queen Elizabeth II in fine style, with many of the shops and houses being attractively decorated for the occasion in 1953. Flags, bunting and shields adorn the frontage of the Co-operative stores in the market place and the notice over the door proclaims that this is, 'Salisbury Co-operative Society Ltd, Wilton Branch'.

For the children, one of the main attractions of Coronation Day in 1953, was the tea party held in the Michael Herbert Hall. In the foreground are the Coronation mugs that were presented to the children, as a memento of the occasion. The day concluded with a torchlight procession to Grovely Down for a bonfire and fireworks display, reviving one of the town's older traditions.

The centre piece of the town's decorations for the Coronation were in the market place in 1953 and they were designed by Horace Uphill. He cleverly used the Pembroke memorial as the centre-piece, covering it with foliage, and placing four shields on it. The crown which topped this was made in his workshop, and when darkness fell it was illuminated with coloured lights, made even more effective by slowly revolving. In the early evening of Coronation Day, a dance was held here as one of the attractions before the bonfire procession.

CORONATION

EIIR

BOROUGH OF WILTON

———

Souvenir

Programme

Programme cover for Coronation celebrations, 1953. In his message to the people of Wilton as part of the coronation celebrations in 1953, the mayor, Alderman V.H. Moore, spoke about how the Elizabethan Pageant to be performed as part of the festivities, would emphasize the changes to the town between the visits of Queen Elizabeth I, and the visit earlier in the year of Queen Elizabeth II. He said it was a visit that the town would remember with pride, and that the town was able to demonstrate that loyalty to the Crown was as firm as ever.

Seven

Around the Town Again

An early view from the top of the Shaftesbury Road in the 1900s, looking down towards Wilton, clearly shows an early form of pavement in front of the houses on the left. Further down on the same side, approximately opposite the person walking on the right, is the house that Edward Slow, the dialect poet, bought after his retirement, naming it 'Elladune', which he believed was Wilton's original name.

The cemetery was consecrated on 19 March 1891 and is situated at the top of the Shaftesbury Road. To the right of the entrance is a small chapel, where funeral services could take place if required. It also had a secondary role as a store for the funeral bier, on which coffins were carried before motorised hearses. It is here that many gypsy families are buried. Wilton witnessed many gypsy funerals in the past, when this bier was used.

The Bell Inn around 1900 stands on the corner of the Wishford and Shaftesbury roads. Today it is minus its railings and modern, heavy traffic thunders by making the exit from the porch quite a hair-raising experience.

This view of the Priory church of St John is taken from the rear, with West Street on the right and the start of the Shaftesbury Road in St John's Square on the other side of the building. This church was attached to the Hospital of St John, founded by Hubert Water, Bishop of Sarum between the years 1189 and 1193. It appears that the original foundation was for a priory and services are still held in the church once a week, usually on a Wednesday morning.

On the right between the trees are the almshouses of the Order of St John and the house just beyond the tree, is the old gatehouse. At this point on West Street in the early 1900s a gate was situated across the road which denoted the end of the town, as the area beyond there was considered to be out of town limits and in the parish of Burcombe. The row of terraced houses on the left, were demolished in the latter part of the twentieth century, making way for a detached house, standing well back from the pavement.

This view of West Street in the 1950s looks back to the gatehouse and the Priory church, with some of the houses in St John's Square clearly visible. Above their rooftops, the downs leading up to Grovely woods are also just visible and from where there is a good view of the town looking down West Street. The row of small terraced houses disappearing off the picture on the right have now been demolished. The site is now Pembroke Court which offers sheltered accommodation for the elderly.

On West Street in the 1950s, looking towards the market place and town hall, on the immediate left is Francis Pretty's ironmongers. This shop stocked all kinds of tools and accessories and nails were sold by the pound weight. Just past the post office is Redwood's Grocery Stores, which although rather on the small side, was always busy. On the right, just below the sign advertising Players Cigarettes, is Snoad's confectioners and tobacconists, which was a very popular shop for children buying their sweets and ice cream.

Viewed from the market place end, West Street in the early 1900s certainly proves that life moved at a more leisurely pace around the turn of the nineteenth century. The shop on the immediate left belonged to W. Bonning, a stationer and bookseller, who also sold postcards of the town. He also encouraged Edward Slow when he first started writing his dialect poems, arranging to have them printed as well as selling them.

The Michael Herbert Hall, which was completed in 1938, was built in memory of Michael Herbert as a venue for social functions. During the 1950s and 1960s it was popular for dances, held there on Saturday nights. The resident orchestra was lead by Charles S. Hart, and other bands from the district played on an occasional basis. These included the popular band from Salisbury, 'The Merry Macs'. The stage was used by local drama groups after the last war, plus for carnival variety shows in the 1950s and 1960s.

The Library on South Street, which was opened in 1951, originally had been the Friends' Meeting House and later a Conservative Club. During the First World War, it became Miss Uphill's dug-out, where soldiers could spend some of their precious leisure hours quietly reading magazines and having refreshments. It became popular with the Australian Forces, many of whom were befriended by Miss Uphill, who even wrote letters to their families on their behalf.

North Street in the late 1940s. On the left is the small shop belonging to Mr Wright, who not only repaired clocks and watches, but sold them as well. Although the shop only had a small interior, it was crammed with watches and clocks of every description and many of the clocks were working. It was fascinating to listen to all those ticking clocks when you entered the shop to be greeted by Mr Wright, who usually appeared from the back room where he did the repairs.

North Street in the early 1900s. Does the clock fixed to the roof of the shop on the left, indicate that the business was selling clocks and watches, or was it merely there to tell people the time? The shop is long gone, as are the railings surrounding the churchyard of St Mary's church on the right. These were removed for metal salvages during the Second World War effort.

On the right is the Six Bells Inn, which in the eighteenth century was a coaching inn, receiving its trade from the Bristol to Salisbury traffic. The 1754 map shows that the stables were situated at the rear. The building on the left, displaying the figure of a horse on the roof, was originally the 'White Horse Brewery', which belonged to Thomas Holly. Later, sometime during the 1920s it became Barratt and Brown, a grocery shop. Today the shop is operated by the Burnbake Trust.

Above: This timber framed house on North Street is reputed to be the oldest house in the town and at the time the photograph was taken it belonged to the Wilton Free School, and was used as the headmaster's residence. The school was next door, set back from the road behind the railings on the left. The school, which was charity based, provided the school master with a salary of £20 per year, a rent-free house and an allowance of £4 per year for the purchase of school stationery and for the heating of the schoolroom during winter months. It is most likely that the house was occupied by Mr Coates, on the date the photograph was taken, who by all accounts was very strict and stood no nonsense from any of the pupils. To ensure the boys always appeared smartly dressed when out in the street, they were provided with a new uniform every Easter.

Opposite above: Keeping law and order in the town in 1951 is PC Nicholas, who was one of the policemen operating from the former police station in the Wilton Road. This was the time when the local police wore cads, rather than the familiar helmets. Behind him is Barton's Food Store and to its left, the fish and chip shop, where fish and chips cost six old pence.

Opposite below: Foyle's Corn, Seed and Fruit Shop was a well established business in North Street around 1935 and it was always very busy. It was noted for its fruit and good quality seeds, remaining in business until around the end of the 1950s. Street renumbering took place in the town around 1950. Note the number change on Foyle's shop from 26 to 82, evident in this photograph.

Above: Lever's the Butchers, *c.* 1935. Lever's the butchers were also a well established family business, which sold good quality meat and had, at this period, their own slaughter house at the rear of the shop. The notice in the centre of the display reads: 'This Window Is Dressed For The *Daily Express* First National Retail Display Challenge Cup. Prizes For Shoppers See Todays *Daily Express*'. Just look at those prices!

Left: At the top end of North Street in the 1950s. Just before Cross Bridge, on the extreme left is the small area that used to be the 'pound', where stray animals would be kept until claimed. Immediately to its right is Pound Meadow, where sheep for the Wilton Sheep fair were kept overnight. Today the sheep come in lorries, so the meadow is no longer used for this purpose.

Workmen are busy attending to the road surface of North Street in the early 1900s. A top layer of tarmac is being laid down in the section of North Street between Cross Bridge and Burdensball Bridge, just before the junction with the Warminster Road.

Demolition of Fancy Row in North Street began in the early 1950s, in order to make way for a new development of council flats on the site. Many of the houses had become run down and were not considered suitable for habitation in the postwar days. The area was considered by some to have become a real eyesore, practically resembling a slum. Interiors were cramped and badly lit, some idea of the last stages of demolition is shown in the photograph.

This view of Fancy Row taken from the North Street end, just before demolition commenced, shows all too clearly how the area had deteriorated. The Fancy Row name derives from the eighteenth century, when inhabitants were employed working from home in the making of fancy waistcoats and elegant linings for gentleman's dress of the period. These workers were poorly paid for their long hours of labour, the only consolation being that they might have been able to collect some financial assistance from the Poor Relief Fund.

Work starting on the first block of flats, situated at the rear of the houses in North Street, soon got under way on completion of the demolition work in the early 1950s. The area was named Churchill Court in honour of Sir Winston Churchill and the builders were Moulding & Sons. In later years Wylye Lodge opened offering sheltered accommodation for the elderly and handicapped.

On Saturday 7 August 1915 there was a remarkable accident at the London and South Western Railway station, when the 11.07 am Exeter express from Salisbury ran into three goods waggons which had been left on the line during shunting operations. This photograph, taken by the author's grandfather, shows the station porter, Mr Ricketts, talking to some of the passengers about his miraculous escape from serious injury, or even death. Prior to the accident he was posting bills on the railings at the Salisbury end of the platform. On hearing the impact and seeing the engine and trucks hurtling towards him, he jumped from the platform onto the permanent way and up onto the opposite platform. Looking back he saw one of the trucks hurled into the air with jets of tar bursting from barrels; which crashed down to the platform within a foot of where he had been working.

The engine is pictured after the crash in 1915, its boiler showing streaks of tar running down the side. Main damage was to the front of the engine, which was repaired and returned to service a few weeks later. The engine, a Drummond T9310, was driven by J. Coombs of Exeter, who was praised by the passengers for his skill in averting a more serious disaster. There was no loss of life and only four people sustained minor injuries, which were treated by a local doctor at the station. All passengers were able to resume their journey later in the day.

The summer of 1947 saw the inauguration of the all Pullman service of the *Devon Belle*, which changed engines at Wilton. Here waiting to take the 'up' *Belle* to Waterloo, is Merchant Navy Class No. 2164, Cunard White Star, resplendent in her Southern livery, complete with the train's nameplate attached to the streamline casing. The engine was built in October 1941 and modified in July 1958.

The 'down' *Belle* arrives at Wilton in around 1948, where the London engine was detached from the train and returned to Sailsbury in reverse. The new engine is waiting in the adjacent siding ready to take over the train for the remainder of its journey to Exeter.

For such a small town, Wilton was unusual because it had two railway stations, the Great Western Railway and London and South Western. The Great Western Railway was the first to arrive in June 1856, followed three years later in 1859 by the London and South Western Railway, at that time known as the Salisbury and Yeovil Railway company. This drawing of the Great Western Railway is a painting from a postcard of the station from the early 1900s.

SOUTHAMPTON, PORTSMOUTH, BRIGHTON, HASTINGS, and SALISBURY, BRISTOL, BATH, EXETER, PLYMOUTH, and the WEST OF ENGLAND,
via SALISBURY.

The London and South Western Railway Company do not guarantee these times being kept, nor do they hold themselves responsible for delay—nor for the connection
between the Trains as shown by these Tables.

DOWN.	WEEK DAYS.								SUNDAYS.				UP.	WEEK DAYS.									SUNDAYS.		
	1 & 2 class	1 & 2 class	1 2 3 class	1 & 2 class	1 & 2 class	1 & 2 class	1 & 2 class	1 & 2 class	1 2 3 class	1 & 2 class	1 & 2 class	1 & 2 class		1 & 2 class	1 & 2 class	1,2,3 class	1 & 2 class	1 & 2 class	1 & 2 class	1 & 2 class	1 & 2 class	noon	1 2 3 class	1 & 2 class	1 & 2 class
	a m	a m	a m	a m	a m	p m	p m	p m	a m	p m	p m	p m		a m	a m	a m	a m	a m	a m	a m	a m	noon	a m	p m	p m
Hastings dep.				6 45						2 0			PLYMOUTH dp.								6 50	12 0			
Brighton..... „				8 30	12 20	2 0	3 2			2 0			Exeter ...... „				7 10				9 55	1 45			
Prismouth ar				10 15	1 25	3 45	4 30			1 40															
Ryde1 W. Mv.	6 40		10 0			1 0	1 20	1 15	2 50		4 15		Bristol ...... „			6 50		11 10			1 45	6 25			
Ptrsmouth. „	8 10		10 50	11 40	2 15	4 15	6 10		8 40		5 10	7 5	Bath ...... „			7 25		11 35			2 20	7 0			
Cosham... „	8 20		11 0	11 50	2 25	4 25	6 40	8 50			5 20	7 15	Bathampln. „			7 10		11 45			2 30	7 8			
Porchester „	8 45		11 6	11 56	2 30		6 40	8 55			5 20	7 15	Bradford „			7 50		12 15			2 50	7 30			
Gosport... „	8 10		11 0	11 50	2 30	4 15	6 40	8 55			5 25	7 20	Trowbridge „			8 0		12 15			3 0	7 45			
Fareham ... „	8 16		11 15	12 5	2 47	4 38	6 55	9 7			5 37	7 35	Westbury „			8 25		12 30			3 20	8 3			
Botley ...... „	8 47		11 25	12 20	3 52	4 48	7 5	9 19			5 47	7 50	Warminster „			8 40		1 5			3 35	8 20			
Bishopstoke ar			11 40	12 40	3 4	4 57	7 20	9 15			6 5	8 11	Heytesbury „			8 50		1 15			3 45	8 30			
Southamptn „	9 20		12 0	12 50	3 10	5 10	7 45	9 55			6 20	8 20	Wilton....... „			9 25		1 50			4 10	9 1			
			1 2 3 1 & 2										SALISBURY. ar.			9 35		2 0			4 25	9 15			
Southampton dp	9 0		11 35	12 45	3 0	4 50	7 10	9 30	1 0			7 45	SALISBURY. dp.	8 0		10 35		2 20		4 0	6 20	9 20	8 31		5 0 6 4
Bishpstoke. dp	9 25		11 55	1 11	3 50	5 10	7 30	9 47	1 25			8 10	Dean.......... „	8 18		10 55				4 18	6 38	9 37	8 50		5 20 7
Chandlr'sFd.„	9 31		12 1	1 18					1 30			8 15	Dunbridge „	8 27		11 2		2 42		4 28	6 48	9 44	9 2		5 27 7
Romsey ...... „	9 42		12 11	1 27	4 5	5 25	7 44	10 0	1 41			8 24	Romsey „	8 30		11 10		2 52		4 38	6 59	9 51	9 15		5 41 8
Dunbridge... „	9 50		12 21	1 37	4 14	5 34	7 53	10 15	1 51			8 36	Chandlr'sFd.„	8 47		11 23					7 10		9 27		
Dean .... „	9 58		12 30	1 46	4 21		8 3	10 25	2 1			8 47	Bishopstoke ar	8 53		11 30		3 10		5 0	7 10	10 0	9 40		6 5 8
SALISBURY. ar	10 15		12 47	2 5	4 40	5 55	8 20	10 45	2 20			9 5	Southampton „			12 0		3 25		5 20	7 45	10 52	10 0		6 30 8
SALISBURY. dp	10 50		1 40		6 5								Southampton dp	6 30	9 0	11 35		2 50	3 10	4 50	7 10		9 35	1 0	7 3
Wilton....... „	10 57		1 50		6 12								Bishopstoke „	6 50	9 15	11 55		3 15	3 35	5 12	7 35	11 20	9 45	1 25	8 1
Heytesbury „	11 31		2 24		6 44								Botley ...... „	7 5	9 30	11 7		3 35	3 52	5 24	7 47	11 36	10 0	1 37	8 2
Warminstr. „	11 43		2 35		6 53								Fareham ... „	7 35	9 41	12 19		3 35	4 15	5 36	7 59	11 50	10 12	1 49	8 3
Westbury „	12 15		3 0		7 15								Gosport..... ar	7 40	9 55	12 35		3 45	4 40	5 50	8 10		10 30	2 3	8 4
Trowbridge „	11 30		3 15		7 30								Porchester dp	7 40	9 50	12 25				4 22		8 6		10 16 1 46	8 4
Bradford ... „	12 40		3 25		7 40								Cosham .... „	7 55	9 59	12 33				4 28		4 8	8 12 10 35	2 1	8 5
Bathampin. „	1 0		3 45		8 0								PORTSMOUTH ar	8 10	10 10	12 46			1 55	4 40	6 0	8 20	10 50	2 15	9 0
Bath......... ar.	1 8		3 55		8 6								Ryde (1 W.) „	9 15	11 10	1 10		4 45		7 35		12 0	1 15		
Bristol....... „	1 35		4 30		8 30								Portsmouth dep	9 15	11 30					4 0		6 15			4 0
Bristol ...dep	3 0		6 0										Brighton ... ar	9 55	1 20					6 20		7 55			6 15
Exeter ...... ar.	6 0		8 31										PLYMOUTH ... „	1 30	4 30					9 50					9 25
PLYMOUTH .. „	9 15		12 0																					

* The Trains will stop at the Stations thus marked by Signal only.
N.B.—The Classes of Carriages have only reference to the Trains
between Salisbury and Southampton or Portsmouth.

Even though the Salisbury and Yeovil Railway had opened their line through Wilton, it was only open as far as Gillingham so through services to Exeter and the West Country were still not possible on this route. Instead to get from Wilton to the West Country meant a long laborious journey on the Great Western Railway route via Bristol. This Great Western Railway timetable from 1859, published by the London and South Western Railway Company, shows just how long a journey from Plymouth to Portsmouth could take. A weekday departure at 6.50am from Plymouth by this round-about route seemed to take forever, not arriving in Portsmouth until 8.25pm in the evening. It also appears that there were only two trains a day, the second leaving at noon, taking twelve hours and twenty five minutes to complete this journey. It is interesting to note, that there were no trains at all through Wilton to Bristol and beyond on a Sunday. When the author was a young boy, there were hardly any trains on this Great Western Railway route on a Sunday, so few in fact that signals on the line through the Wylye Valley were set to clear all the day and no signalmen were on duty. They finished on Saturday night and didn't return until the first trains on Monday morning.

This photograph of Wilton House was most probably taken in the early part of the nineteenth century, taken from across the River Nadder which flows through its beautiful grounds. The house was built on the site of Wilton Abbey, its grounds were granted by Henry VIII in 1539, at the dissolution of the abbey, to William Herbert, the first Earl of Pembroke, whose family were of Welsh origin.

This view in the 1940s shows the part of the house that faces the lawns leading to its extensive gardens on the south side. The house has had many connections with royalty and famous people during its four hundred years. Charles I was a regular visitor and Shakespeare performed here, before James I, in the comedy, *As You Like It*, which he wrote for the occasion and where the play received its first performance in 1603.

The Double Cube room, which has been called the finest proportioned room in England, remains exactly the same today as when it was built. It measures sixty feet long by thirty feet wide and thirty feet high. It is so-called because it is double the size of the adjoining room which is a perfect cube. Designed by Inigo Jones and completed by Webb, around 1653, the walls are pine panelled and elaborately decorated with swags of fruit, flowers, foliage, draperies, ciphers and coronets, all gilded in different shades of gold. It was used in the seventeenth and eighteenth centuries as a dining room, and in the nineteenth and twentieth centuries as a sitting room and ballroom. Kings and Queens of England including George III and Queen Charlotte as well as sovereigns from many foreign countries have sat and danced in it. During the Second World War, when the house became the headquarters of Southern Command, the Double Cube room became a major operations centre for the planning of the D-Day operations. In those times both General Eisenhower and Winston Churchill made frequent visits, arriving by the back entrance at the sawmills in South Street. The paintings in the room were carefully protected, covered with maps of the beaches of France, and behind the walls of the grounds many secret exercises took place.

Henry, 9th Earl of Pembroke had a real interest in the arts and was an architect. His chief claim to fame is the construction of the beautiful Palladian bridge across the River Nadder. Together with Roger Morris, his clerk of works at the time, he designed the bridge, but in order to complete the task Henry destroyed the de Caux formal garden and altered the course of the river; landscaping the garden in the prevailing fashion. The bridge was completed in 1737.

This picture shows the rear of Wilton church, seen from the meadow which adjoins it. At the base of the semi-circular section is the crypt built as a burial vault for the Earls of Pembroke. The crypt was divided into three compartments by two, three-bay arcades and reached by an outer barrel-vaulted vestibule which was lit by two cruciform windows. The walls of the crypt are decorated with five figurative marble reliefs of the sixteenth and seventeenth century surrounded by marble framing and bosses.

Picturesque WILTSHIRE.
Wilton Church

This painting of Wilton church from the late nineteenth century, with a view from across the river at Castle Meadow, depicts the church in a truly rural setting with the skyline dominated by the ten foot bell tower. Although there has been growth in the foliage over the years, the church is still visible from this viewpoint.

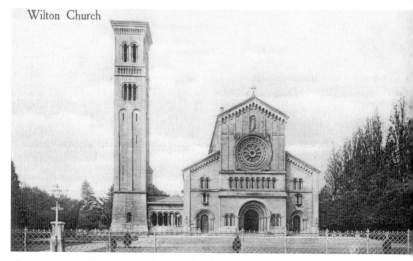

Wilton Church

The church was built between 1841 and 1845 and was a gift of Lord Herbert of Lea. It was built in the Northern Lombardic style, inspired by the Lombardic churches of St Pietro and Santa Maria, near Viterbo, north of Rome. Its orientation is unusual in that it is on a north-south axis, alleged to have been the wish of the Dowager Countess of Pembroke, as this was the custom in her native Russia. It is seen here around the turn of the nineteenth century.

The altar lies behind the Lady Chapel of Wilton Church, which is made mainly of oak and was a gift from the inhabitants of Wilton. Above is a beautiful mosaic depicting Christ in Glory, attended by the blessed Virgin Mary and St Nicholas, and is in memory of Canon Dacres Olivier, who was Rector of the Wilton Parish for nearly fifty years. The work was executed by Miss Gertrude Martin, who used twenty pieces of mosaic in each eyeball of the Christ figure. She also worked on the Pembroke mosaic in the forefront. This was made in memory of Sidney, 14th Earl of Pembroke, his wife and younger son, Hon. George Herbert. During the time she was working on the Pembroke mosaic, Miss Martin broke her hip on two occasions, but after recovery, mounted the ladder daily in order to complete the work. The marble pillars supporting the arch, come from the Temple of Venus at Porto Venereon in the Gulf of Spezia, built by the Roman Consul; Lucius Porcius Licinius in 151 BC.

Looking towards the main entrance in West Street, above the gallery is the Wheel Window, which mainly contains glass brought back as loot to Paris by Napolean. Details of the Wilton Charities are inscribed in the arches above and below the gallery, and the words carved across the gallery read: 'All things come of Thee, and of Thineown have we given Thee', and were chosen by Sidney Herbert who refused to have his name inscribed, despite ordering the church to be built.

The Rectory on West Street in the early 1900s. This fine georgian building in West Street from the early 1900s is of deep red brick and was built here before the church. It was thought to have been built around 1790 by the owner of a factory which once stood on the site of the present community centre. This view of the rear of the rectory shows the layout of the garden nearest the house, beyond which was orchard land. The house is no longer a rectory; but is privately owned and known as St Andrew's House.

The Congregational church, shown here in the early 1900s, was situated in Crow Lane and is dated 1791; the time of its rebuilding. It was the largest non-conformist church in the town and in 1829 was reputed to have had four hundred members. It thrived through the nineteenth century but there was a decline in attendances during the twentieth, resulting in its closure in the mid 1980s. It has been converted into four flats.

Members of the Congregational church entered into the carnival spirit with their entry during the 1950s as 'Happy Families'. The gentleman wearing the top hat is Leonard Jukes, Sunday School superintendent. His wife, also a Sunday School teacher, can be seen fourth from left, third row up, and their daughter Marcia, front row fourth from right. The tableau was based on the popular card game of the same name.

The Congregational Sunday School, around 1938 possibly when the Revd Edgar Stephen Perry took over the ministry of the church in 1938. He remained as minister until late in 1944. Revd Perry can be seen on the extreme right.

Parties for pensioners are always a popular event as this one, held at the Michael Herbert Hall around 1966, shows. It was most likely arranged by Huw Aubrey in one of his mayoral years, who ensured that the elderly had a good time during Christmas festivities. Huw Aubrey is pictured on the extreme right and was mayor in 1966 and 1967.

The bell ringers of Wilton church are pictured outside the church, by the entrance leading to the bell tower in 1950. They are from left to right, back row: J. Oakley, G.T. Hibberd, B. Lever, -?- A. Hainse. Front row: H. Roper, J. Kiddie, A. Trimby and J. Brown. The identity of the little boy is not known.

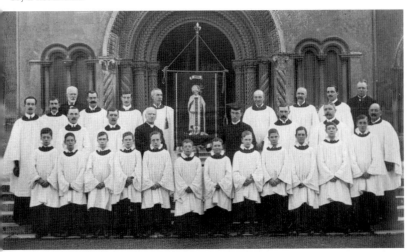

The Wilton church choir during the 1900s. The gentleman on the left, dressed in black, is Canon Dacres Olivier. To his right, wearing the 'mortar board' hat, is the Revd Barrington-Brown, who was possibly the curate at the time.

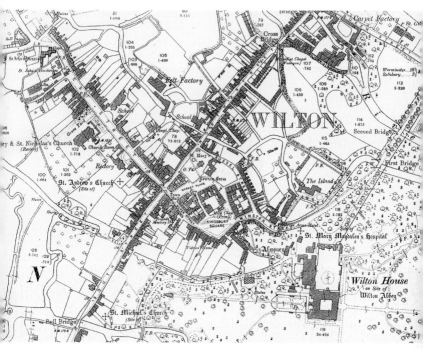

This 1900s map shows exactly how the town looked at the beginning of the twentieth century. Many landmarks shown are still familiar in Wilton one hundred years on. There are some which have now totally disappeared, but they are surprisingly very few. These include the Wesleyan chapel at the top of North Street, the Free School also in North Street and the National School in West Street, but their buildings still remain in use today.

Eight

People

There was quite a stir in Wilton in March 1912, when five of its sons decided to emigrate to Canada to seek their fortunes. They received a great send-off when they left the town by train. The men were Mr Fry, A.S. Randall, B. Croome, E. Grant and J. Farrant, but not necessarily in this order.

Although not a resident of Wilton, Mrs Eliza Goulden of Bowerchalke, is worth a mention as she celebrated her 100th birthday in 1912, the same year as a Wilton resident celebrated hers (see below). It would seem that South Wiltshire was a healthy area in which to live, as it was a rare occurrence for two people, who lived not too far apart, to reach this age.

In September 1912, Mrs Hannah Blake, a resident of Wilton, celebrated her 100th birthday. Born in Dinton in 1812, the exact date of her birth wasn't known but the baptismal register, the only real proof of age in those days, revealed that she was baptised with her twin sister in December 1812. Coming to Wilton at an early age, she was employed by a Mr Woodstock of Fugglestone House. She married James Blake at Fugglestone church, who was a coal merchant.

Canon Dacres Olivier during the late 1800s. Canon Olivier was Rector of the parishes of Wilton and Netherhampton for fifty-two years, and was a man with a great sense of ecclesiastical dignity. He was determined that the old ways of the church should continue, insisting that two clergymen should assist at the Sunday services in Wilton Church. However, he did constantly think of new ways for the Church to work, but keeping within a budget was not a strong point, and nothing would induce him to do so. Often, when the parish magazines published the annual accounts, it was recorded that the small balances were paid by the Rector himself. In his private life certain living standards were maintained, but the Rector also strained these expenses to the limit. He retired from his duties in September 1912.

Edith Olivier, the daughter of Canon Olivier, shown here around 1912, was born at Wilton Rectory in 1872 and was one of eight children in a family that was very close. Although she was a parson's daughter, she had a rare and worldly wit. Later in life she became a writer of many books, an antiquarian and a town councillor, through which she achieved the honour of becoming Wilton's first lady mayor. She never married, but when living at Daye House in Wilton park, she often entertained her many friends including Siegfried Sassoon, the painter Rex Whistler, composer William Walton and Sir Cecil Beaton, as well as many others. She was a much loved person among the people of the town.

Due to his unselfish efforts in trying to save the life of a friend, who had fallen over a parapet at Bulbridge into a swollen river at midnight in December 1911, James Henry Sanger became a local hero. Although unsuccessful in his attempt, suggestion was made in the local press that his efforts should be rewarded. At a ceremony for the opening of the Recreation Ground in May 1912, Lord Pembroke gave various testimonials to his good character. These were accompanied by a bronze medal and a certificate from the Royal Humane Society. Next came a watch in heavy double-cased silver, suitably inscribed and finally, a silver cup from the Master and members of Mr Courtenay Tracy's Otter Hunt, of which James was an employee.

Born in Quidhampton, William James Lane, pictured here in 1891, was employed at the Wilton Carpet Factory as a weaver, where he served as an employee for no fewer than fifty years. Ill-health forced him to retire in 1926, at which time he had risen to a responsible position with the company. Outside his employment he showed a practical interest in many activities of the town. He was associated with the Oddfellows Friendly Society, becoming Grand Master of the lodge in 1891 and Provincial Grand Master of the Salisbury district in 1902. His other interests included, Secretary of the Wilton Total Abstinence Society, Wilton Cycling Club, treasurer and sometime auditor of Wilton United Football Club. At the time of his death in 1931, he was treasurer of the Old Weaver's Club.

Born in Wilton, Samuel Jacobs resided here until sixteen years of age when, having completed his education, he was offered and accepted a responsible post in the London offices of a large mercantile firm. He remained there for a number of years, in his spare time he acquainted himself with learning shorthand. He took a position of assistant town clerk in the borough of Croydon, and during the illness and deaths of two former town clerks, had great responsibilities thrust upon him, which he carried out to the great satisfaction of the council and the inhabitants of the borough.

Businessman John White, pictured here in 1897, owned a chain of grocery shops, one of which was situated in North Street and proved to be very successful, attracting much business through unusual window displays. A member of the town council, he held the office of mayor on no less than six occasions, 1897-98, 1903-4 and 1904-5. He was clever with his business advertisements. The people, horses and carriages were drawn out of proportion to the size of his shop behind them, in the illustration. The idea was that it made his shop look much larger than it actually was!

YES !

· · · · · · · · IT IS SO.

· ·

FOR THE BEST PLACE IN THE DISTRICT

TO OBTAIN GOOD VALUE IN

TEAS, →:|C:|←

GROCERIES,

╫AND╫ PROVISIONS,

GO TO

J. WHITE,

North St., WILTON.

Whites Grocery Stores advertisements in 1898. This advertisement was published in a Wilton guide of 1898 and is one of John White's earlier advertisements, which is simpler than many of the ones in later periods. The business was owned later by the International, until closure in the later part of the nineteenth century. It is now the premises of the Home Decorator.

Nine

Wilton Moments

Warminster Road around the turn of the nineteenth century. This road is the now notorious A36. Not a car in sight here and it is perfectly safe for the photographer to set up his tripod in the middle of the road to take this picture of workmen by the roadside. It is even safe enough for the mother to walk her child on the outside of the pavement.

This bridge at Bulbridge in the early 1900s, is situated at the end of South Street and passes over the River Nadder just before the river runs through Wilton Park. This is the bridge mentioned in the previous section, where the friend of James Sanger fell over the parapet and was drowned. As one can see, the parapet was very low, but the bridge was widened during the 1950s and the parapet made higher for improved safety.

The Wilton Arms during the late 1800s was a public house situated in West Street, near to the market place end of the street. The premises is still plying the same trade today, but is now known as the Bear Inn, and during the twentieth century appears to have changed very little. Even the modern sign is fixed to the wall in the same position as the one in the picture.

This day in August 1920 appears to have been fine and sunny when some workers of the Wilton Carpet Factory took a trip to Bournemouth. These vehicles were known in those days as charabancs and this one was hired from Rowland and Sons, Castle Street, Salisbury.

This group of gentlemen gathered on Cross Bridge in North Street, are members of the Wilton Cycling Club from the early 1920s.

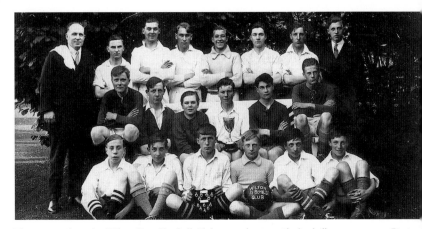

Three teams from the Wilton Boys Football Club entered a six-a-side football tournament at Devizes in 1931. The team in the centre row, were successful in winning the cup. The top and bottom rows were not successful, although the bottom row did manage to win a shield. Left to Right, back row: Mr Jeans, Chuck Cooper, Reg Wilton, Hubert James, Frank Weeks Bill Humphries, Harry Noyce and Eric Blake. Middle row: Sid Trim, Jumbo Binden, Chippy Scott, -?-, Fred Ricketts and Jack Cope. Bottom row: Ken Saunders, Charlie Furnell, Harry Ricketts, Jack Smith, Eddy Dimmer and Charlie Morris.

Wilton Wednesday Football Club, 1911-12. This club was successful in reaching the final of the Salisbury Wednesday Cup and a semi-final of the Shaftesbury tournament in 1911-12. From left to right, back row: F. Down, A. Chivers, A. Moore, R. Saunders, A. Hinton A. Morris and L. Hinton, (Chairman). Front row: C. Jenvy, A Remain, (Captain) L. Parsons, F. Robinson and J. Underwood, (Hon. Sec).

What a splendid car! Out for a drive in Wilton in around 1900.

An idyllic summer scene in Castle Meadow almost one hundred years ago, shows some children of the town relaxing by the River Wylye in glorious summer sunshine. In the centre background, the arch of the bridge carrying the London and South Western Railway line over the river, west of Wilton is just visible.

Agricultural shows have always been a popular event for firms selling farm machinery. This one in the 1930s concerned the managing director of Brewers of Wilton in Ewart Lane, He is taking an opportunity to discuss the advantages of one of the company's latest products to some prospective buyers.

Established by Albert Brewer in the early 1860s as a blacksmiths, Brewers soon progressed to repairing farm machinery as part of the business. In 1902 the company was sold and the new owner made great changes, devoting the main part to selling agricultural machinery specifically for the farming community. This photograph was most likely taken soon after the new owner took over.

Wilton's ARP Wardens First Aid Section, in the early 1940s. The First Aid Section was only one part of the formation of Wilton's ARP Wardens, who played an important part during the Second World War in helping to protect the town. They looked out for enemy planes and fires in case bombs should be dropped, plus insuring that blackout regulations were very strictly observed. In 1943 the Chief Warden was Percy Hare, a local wheelwright and undertaker, who was also one of the people who took part in a wartime broadcast from the town.

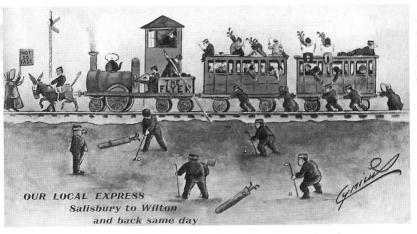

Although this cartoon could have been produced nationally at the time the railway was opening up all over the country, it appears that Wilton jumped on the bandwaggon to use this popular version to the town's advantage c. 1856. More than likely it refers to the opening of the Great Western Railway station in 1856.

On 6 May 1939 the former parish church was re-hallowed with great ceremony and here the choir, of the parish church in West Street, enter in procession through the ruins of the church. A great many of the townspeople turned out to witness this very unique occasion.

The ceremony of re-hallowing was conducted by the Bishop of Salisbury, Dr Neville Lovett. During the ceremony, a memorial tablet was dedicated to Robert Bingham, Bishop of Salisbury, who was installed here in 1229 and to Robert Bingham, the US Ambassador. Having discovered his ancestor's connection he offered to restore the building as a memorial to him. It was unveiled by Rt Hon. George Charles Bingham.

In the 1871 census, Joseph Ward is listed as a linen draper, living above his shop in North Street. His two daughters, Mary and Jane were employed as shop assistants in their father's shop. Today the first section of the shop is occupied by Barclays Bank, while the rear section is Keith's, the ladies hairdressers.

The ceremony of beating the bounds dates back to very early times in history, when parish boundaries were regularly defined by this procedure. This revival, in 1952, shows the party assembled at the Market Cross, prior to their walk round the parish boundary. Leading the walkers on this occasion, holding one of the boundary maps, is Mr G.C. Moody, who was the Mayor at this time. To his right, wearing plus fours is the Revd William Drury, Rector of Wilton and the tall gentleman immediately behind him to his left, is the Revd John James Haynes, minister of the Congregational church in Crow Lane. The two boys on the extreme right, holding sticks are Douglas Norris and, in the dark blazer, is Philip Boon. The sticks were used to ceremonially beat the boys when a corner of the boundary was reached. Not only did the walk take place along roads but meadows and farmer's fields were crossed in defining the old boundary.

Right: A Wilton shepherd in 1938. Sheep were once a familiar sight on the Wiltshire Downs around the town.

Below: A sheep fair in Wilton around the 1930s. Sheep fairs in Wilton have been an institution for hundreds of years, but only commenced on the present site in 1775. In 1893 it was recorded that 40,000 sheep passed through the fairs in that year, but at the end of the September fair in 1901, it was estimated that between 9,000 and 10,000 sheep were penned. The use of wattle hurdles to pen the sheep only ceased about 1989-90.

Left: Dinner time down on the farm, *c.* 1938. This sheep is receiving special attention from its shepherd!

Below: Grovely church in the early 1900s served a small community of Wilton estate workers, that lived in the woods in the area near to Grovely Lodge. A small farm was also established and in the 1850s four pairs of cottages were built for farm workers and gamekeepers. There was also a small school where the children received their education, saving them the long walk to Wishford. During the 1950s the community dwindled to nothing and the church and the school were demolished.

The small hamlet of Ugford is situated on the main A36 Shaftesbury road, west of the old boundary stone of the town, just past the cemetery. It lies in a dip on either side of the main road, consisting of only a few houses and a small farm. The lane leaving the main road on the left by the thatch topped wall, leads down to the beautiful water meadows, through which flows the twisting River Nadder.

Munition workers, in the early 1940s. During the Second World War many women were employed as 'war workers' as all able-bodied men were enlisted in the services. This group of munitions workers was photographed by the post office building at Churchfields, Salisbury in the early 1940s, where they were engaged in making two-pound practice bombs for the Royal Navy.

Wesleyan Sunday School,

WILTON.

HYMNS

TO BE SUNG BY THE CHILDREN AT THE 92nd

ANNIVERSARY

OF THE ABOVE SCHOOL ON

SUNDAY, JULY 9, 1893.

SERMONS WILL BE PREACHED BY

MR. S. J. M. MOODY,

OF SALISBURY.

MORNING AT 10.30. EVENING AT 6 O'CLOCK.

ON MONDAY, JULY 10,

A ∴ PUBLIC ∴ TEA ∴ AND ∴ MEETING

WILL BE HELD.

Collection at each Service in aid of the School Funds.

WILTON :
WILTON PRINTING WORKS, NORTH STREET.

THE MOUNT, WILTON

Above: The Mount, King Street, early 1900s. During the 1800s, this was the home of James Edward Nightingale, a bachelor, who lived here with his sister. He was a regular contributor to the *Wiltshire Archaeological Magazine*, writing on many subjects. These included, the *History of Church Plate of Wilts and Dorset*, articles on the succession of the Abesses of Wilton and notes on Wilton seals. Between 1840 and 1872, he was Mayor no less than six times and was partly responsible for designing the mayor's chain which is still in use to this day. When it ceased to be a private house, it was at one time the Wilton Country Hotel, after which it became offices for a local company selling gaming machines. During the late 1990s the house was demolished to make way for a small private housing development, known as Kingsgate.

Opposite: Sunday School Anniversary, 1893. The Wesleyan Methodists were completely separate from the Primitive Methodists, who had their church in Kingsbury Square. The Wesleyan Methodist chapel was very small and situated at the top end of North Street, the site now occupied by a private house known as the Old Chapel, on the corner leading into Riverside Terrace. The building, for the most part, still retains much of the original brickwork and outline of the original building.

Left: Mr Smith, chauffeur to the Earl of Pembroke, is dressed up as Henry VIII ready for a performance in a large pageant that took place on the lawns of Wilton house as a two day celebration for the tercentenary of George Herbert, Rector of Bemerton in 1933. The pageant consisted of four separate episodes, each containing several scenes, and taking about three hours to perform. The event also included a seventeenth-century fair, which was set between the main gates and the house. The organisers took a great deal of care to reproduce items as near as possible to those of the period.

Below: In the early 1900s the small shop next door to White's the Grocers was redeveloped as a double-frontage shop; which also sold groceries. It was owned by ARchie SHeppard, who stayed in business until his retirement around the late 1908s. Today the premises are occupied by the Post Office

North Street, Wilton.

Published by R. Wilkinson & Co., Trowbri
Sold by W. Boning, Wilton.

Throughout its long history, Wilton has received many royal visitors. Here the Prince of Wales on Wednesday 23 May 1923 in a Rolls Royce Landaulette is driven by the Earl of Pembroke's chauffeur, Mr Smith. The prince is being driven past a group of children from the National School in West Street.

Mrs Bessie Partridge, who owned the newsagents in North Street, is shown with her daughter Mary, prior to taking part in a procession to celebrate the Coronation of King George VI in 1937.

Written on the back of this photograph is, 'The Rogues Gallery! Auxiliary Fire Brigade at the Works. It turns out that the 'works' was Fugglestone House, which during the Second World War housed the town council, the head office of the Red Cross and the Auxiliary Fire Service, and was the main centre for the distribution of ration books. The house has long been demolished and the site is now used as the officer's mess of the headquarters of the Land Forces.

These men were members of the Auxiliary Fire Service, formed in 1939 and were in force until the end of the war in 1945, during which time they played an important role in fighting fires and assisting regular crews. The picture was taken in Silver Street and part of Kingsbury Square can be seen in the background.

Right: Gertrude, Countess of Pembroke is portrayed in her wedding dress on the day of her wedding. She was married in Westminster Abbey 19 August 1874 to George Robert Charles, 13th Earl of Pembroke. Formerly, the Countess was Lady Gertrude Francis Talbot, a daughter of the 18th Earl of Shrewsbury. It is reported that all of Wilton celebrated the wedding in great style. The Earl of Pembroke died without issue and was succeeded by his brother Sidney.

Below: The sidings adjacent to the sheep fair field at the southern station, were often put to use for stabling ambulance trains overnight during the Second World War. These trains carried wounded servicemen from the front line. Many of the walking wounded wore a special blue uniform. Here the nursing personnel and a doctor with a dog at his feet, along with other male members of the crew, take time out to pose on the platform by the Red Cross Ambulance Train in around 1943.

Leonard Jukes, shown here in the late 1960s, was the son of the printer, W. Jukes. The family came to Wilton in the late 1800s, to take over the former Wilton and Tisbury Printing Works in North Street. Eventually, Leonard took over the business, remaining until his retirement in 1980. He was a well known figure in the town, taking a keen interest in town activities, including being an active member of the Congregational church in Crow Lane, singing in the choir as well as being the Sunday School Superintendent.

Above: In 1946 the formation of the Wilton Musical and Dramatic Society took place, where at the inaugural meeting, they made ambitious plans to perform two productions a year. Such was the success of the society, they were able to boast a membership of ninety. Here the cast are taking a bow after a performance of Noel Coward's play, *This Happy Breed*, performed at the Michael Herbert Hall.

Opposite below: The cast of this play, entitled, *Aunt Flo's Day Out*, have every reason to be looking happy, as they were successful in winning a gold medal for their performance in the late 1940s. The play was performed by some members of the Wilton Mothers' Union, who took part with other branches in the diocese. The cast are, from left to right: Mrs Simmonds (author), Miss Olivier, Mrs Rosa Harper, Mrs Billy Moore (producer) Mrs M. Colville, Mrs Blandford, Mrs White, Mrs Furnell and Mrs Hubert.

In the year following the formation of the Wilton Historical Society, November 1977, a series of exhibitions depicting the town's history were launched at weekends during August in the council chamber. At this exhibition a few years later, committee members from left to right: Mr Tim Morland, Mrs May Kiddie, and Mr John Boulter, examine one of the old documents that were to be displayed.

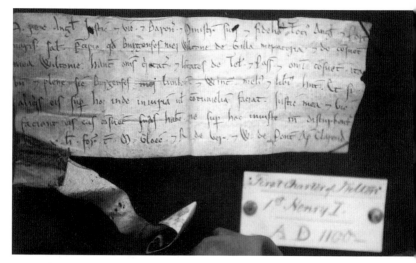

Among the many items that were displayed at the Historical Society exhibitions, were the Wilton Charters. The town was granted fifteen throughout its long history. Illustrated here is the first charter, granted by Henry I in the year 1100 which, when exhibited, always causes great interest.

One of Wilton's main attractions during the Christmas period, is the display of lights on its famous Christmas Tree in the market place. The first lighting was organized by Jack Kiddle, pictured here in the 1950s with the Borough Surveyor. In these early times, Jack had to physically climb the tree to put the star, which was made of iron, on the top of the tree. Today the task of hanging the lights and positioning the star is done by the Wilton fire brigade, who have volunteered their services for a number of years, making it a much safer operation.

On the first Sunday of September 1989, a commemorative service and parade was held in Wilton by the 94th Field Regiment, Royal Artillery Old Comrades; who at the beginning of the Second World War took up stations here to begin intensive training. Soon after becoming a first class fighting unit, the regiment was moved to the expected invasion area of East Kent in 1940. With the hospitality and friendship shown in those early days by Wiltonians, who are still fondly remembered by the Old Comrades, they decided to celebrate their 50th anniversary by once again marching through Wilton. Proudly displaying their medals, the Old Comrades marched from the parish church along West Street.

Ten

Last Look Back

A walk to Grovely Woods, early 1900s. From the path to Grovely Woods a good view of the town can be observed. The field in which cows can be seen is now occupied by council houses, whose gardens took up part of the field. The remainder was used as allotments. The spire of Salisbury Cathedral can be seen dominating the skyline in the far distance.

The tower of St Mary's church in the market place can be seen in the background. The church was in ruins soon after closure in 1845, but this photograph is from the early 1900s.

Warminster Road in the early 1900s was a place of carefree motoring on what is now the very busy A36 through Wilton. It was a time when the motorist did not have to worry too much about oncoming traffic speeding round the bend outside the Wheatsheaf.

It is thought the Wilton Rifle Brigade was originally formed around the time of the Napoleonic Wars, according to Cllr J.M. Swayne who was speaking at the their annual meeting given by the town council in 1912. (These dinners first took place in 1860.) In 1911 they changed to a Territorial Unit, becoming Company of the 4th Battalion Wiltshire Regiment. In the 1870s schools were instructed that all pupils should he given periods of drill, which is supported by the log book of the National School in 1875, revealing that the pupils were being instructed by a Sgt Moon of the Wilton Volunteer Rifle Brigade. In 1912 they were commanded by Capt. Robert Hastings Kendall and the Colour Sgt was W. Hibberd.

Sgt Oswald E. Habel, was one of the many Australian soldiers who came to Salisbury Plain for training in front line duties in 1917. Off duty hours were spent sightseeing and here in Wilton he was befriended by the author's family and on this occasion he had cycled to Wishford with the author's grandfather, who took this picture of him holding a local girl, with Wishford church in the background. He left the following words in an autograph album on 12 August 1917 'Look not upon the past it is no more! Make the most of today it is thyne! Grasp the future with a firm hand'. Sgt Habel survived the war and died peacefully at home in Australia, in 1953.